LEARN THE
A - Z OF WORD
JUGGLING AT OUR
COPYWRITING
CLASS

CULTURECODE
The virtual creativity school

www.culturecode.courses

CONTENTS

Cover Image Credit: X3M Ideas, Lagos, Nigeria

From Africa with Love

Many Africans, especially those from the bigger countries like Nigeria, get so pained when people from other parts of the world say someone is from Africa or going to Africa. They feel the fact that Africa is a mega continent is lost on them.

Indeed, Africa is huge - 54 recognized independent countries with a total land mass of over 30 million Km^2. Africa is 3 times the size of Europe and has a population of over 1.2 billion, second only to Asia in both land mass and population. So, it is understandable that people are furious when they're made to feel they come from a small town. No one likes being belittled. But then, clinging zealously to artificial national boundaries at the expense of trade and development is also the bane of Africa.

When we launched Pitcher Awards in 2018 as another step in the over 12 years' journey of CHINI Africa to promote creativity, the goals were simple. Firstly, to create a regional benchmark for quality and secondly to create visibility and appreciation for African ideas in the global space.

Strangely, organized advertising has been practiced in many parts of Africa for about a century, but the profession did not progress in a way that evolved industry structures for peer evaluation, benchmarking and innovation. This is what a good award system should do. It is not just about winning. For many entrant companies, especially those in Media and PR, submitting work for Pitcher Awards has been a real eye-opener. It was their first opportunity to critically review the brief, analyze the ideas and strategies and present their results in a format they could share with others. They were doubtlessly thankful for the opportunity and the positive changes it could bring to their processes.

The work that you will see in this showcase are basically materials created in West Africa. However, we are opening entries for all materials created or implemented anywhere in Africa from the 2020 edition, taking us another step further in our mission of truly promoting the Creativity of Africa. Indeed, we find no logical justification for restricting entries from anywhere in Africa as the borders are largely artificial. For instance, Nigeria has over 500 different tribes and languages and those tribes are probably just as different from each other as they will be compared to another tribe in say Congo or Mozambique.

We remain thankful to the 3 different juries that judged the works in this volume. The Heritage jury looked at work in traditional categories such as film, print and audio. The Channel jury handled categories including media, PR and integrated campaigns while the Innovation jury were saddled with the responsibility of judging categories in digital, social media and mobile. Each of these pieces selected by the juries represents the will of the team behind them to rise above obstacles by using their creative ingenuity to overcome tough business challenges. Above all, we hope you discover in each work the very passion and love the creators have poured into making them. Enjoy!

Nnamdi Ndu
CEO CHINI Africa

USE OF MEDIA

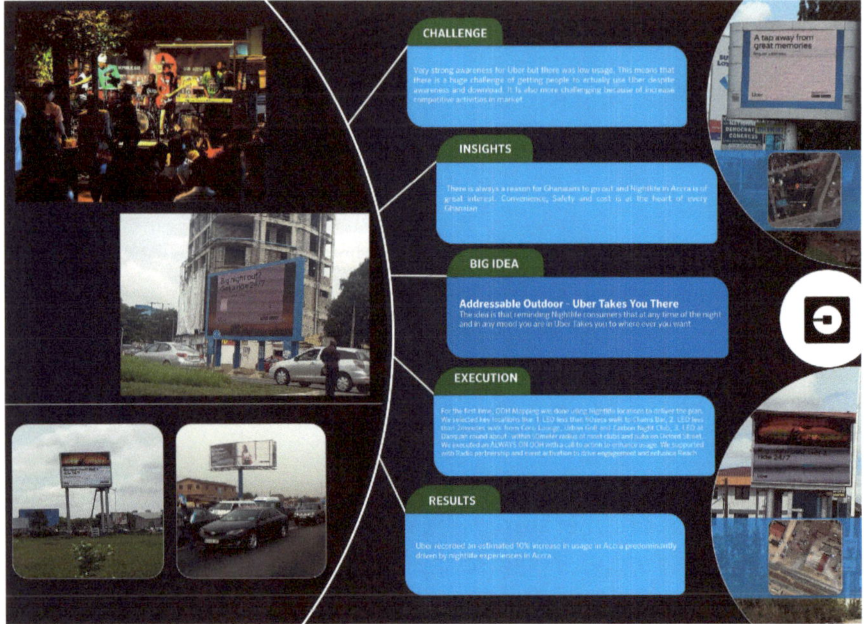

CLIENT   **Uber**

AGENCY   **mediaReachOMD**

AWARD   **Gold**

Addressable Outdoor- Uber Takes You There

CREDITS

Safo Mallet - Planner
OMD

Jerfferson Sowah - OOH Strategist
OMD

Percy Tweneboah - Head of Operations
OMD

Background

The tech transport competition has become very strong in Ghana with the entry of brands like Taxify that has become very aggressive in recruiting drivers and converting riders. Overall, Uber has a very strong awareness but the biggest challenged being faced before this campaign was low usage. This means that there is a huge challenge in getting people to actually use Uber despite awareness and download. It is also more challenging because of the increased competitive activities in media.

Strategy

The strategy was predominantly driven by key insights that there is always a reason for a Ghanaian to go out and Nightlife in Accra is of great interest. The expert community in Accra is also very active and it reflects in the very series of night life experiences that exist in Ghana. Our strategy was to leverage Night life experiences and be there at the point of intrigue to drive conversion. Hence our approach to enhance the use of OOH location programmatically selected through Google maps to deliver call to action at key nightlife locations in Accra

Execution

For the first time, OOH mapping was done using Nightlife locations to deliver the plan. We selected key locations like: 1. LED less than 60secs walk from Charms Bar, 2. LED at Danquah Round About- within a 50 meters radius of most clubs and pubs on Oxford Street, 3. LED less than 2 minutes walk from Coco Lounge, Urban Grill and Carbon Night Club. We executed an ALWAYS ON OOH with a call to action to enhance usage. We supported with Radio partnership and event activation in collaboration with key radio stations to drive engagement and enhance Reach for the campaign

Results

Uber recorded an estimated 10% increase in usage in Accra predominantly driven by nightlife experiences.

USE OF MEDIA

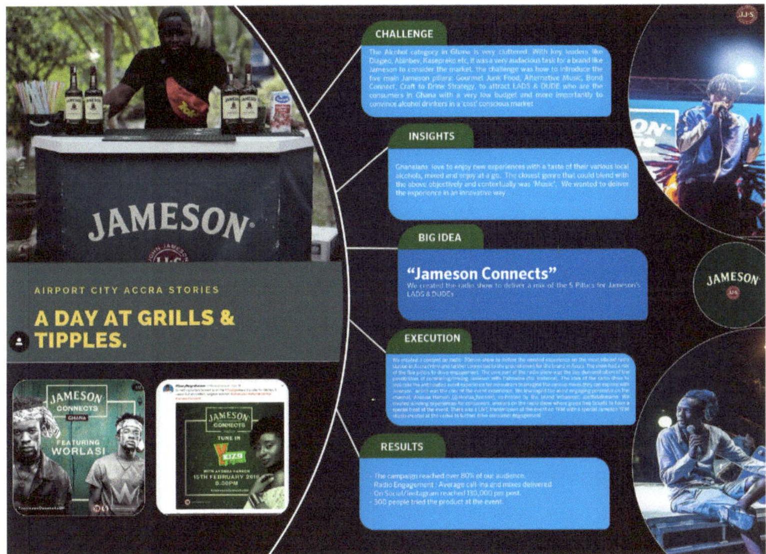

I James Connect Radio

CREDITS

Taniya Mondal Business - Unit Director
OMD

Michael Jacquaye - Planner
OMD

Agatha Animam - Buyer
OMD

Millicent Abudu - Planner
OMD

Deji Adeniji - Content Producer
Eureka Media

CLIENT I **Pernod Ricard**   AGENCY I **mediaReachOMD**   AWARD I **Silver**

Background

The Alcohol category in Ghana is very cluttered. With key leaders like Diageo, Abinbev, Kasepreko etc, it was a very audacious task for a brand like Jameson to consider the market. the challenge was how to introduce the five main Jameson pillars: Gourmet Junk Food, Alternative Music, Bond Connect, Craft to Drink Strategy, to attract LADS & DUDE who are the consumers in Ghana with a very low budget and more importantly to convince alcohol drinkers in a 'cost' conscious market

Strategy

Ghanians love to enjoy new experiences with a taste of their various local alcohol, mixed and enjoy on at the go. The closest that could blend with the above objectively and contextually was 'Music'. We wanted to deliver the core brand essence and experiences leveraging on music in an innovative way- While Music serves as the core, we create opportunities to leverage the key five pillars for the brand on the show

Execution

We created content on radio- 30mins show to deliver the needed experience on the most vibrant radio station in Accra (YFM) and further connected to the ground event for the brand in Accra. The show had a mix of the five pillars to drive engagement. The core part of the radio show was the live demonstration of the possibilities of combining/mixing Jameson with Palmwine (for instance). The idea of the radio show to replicate the anticipated event experience for consumers to imagine the various mixes they can explore with Jameson- which was the core of the event experience. We leveraged the most engaging presenter on the channel; Akosua Hanson (@akosua_hanson); co hosted by the brand influencer; @officialkwame. We created winning experiences for consumers. winners on the radio show where given free tickets to have a special treat at the event. There was a LIVE transmission of the event on YFM with a special Jameson YFM studio created at the venue to further drive consumer engagement

Results

The campaign delivered 80% of the target audience

Radio engagement: Average call in and mixes delivered

On social/instagram reach 130,000 per post

About 300 consumers had a taste of the different option of the Jameson mixes at the event

USE OF MEDIA

Budweiser FIFA WORLD CUP

CREDITS

Ola Olowo - CCO/MD
Isobar

Oluwatobi Alabi - Digital Manager
Iprospect

Joshua Oyeleye - Media Strategy Manager
Vizeum

Franscoe Bouwer - Marketing Manager
ABInBev

Olajumoke Okikiolu - Connections Marketing Manager
ABInBev

CLIENT | **ABInBev**   **AGENCY** | **Vizeum Nigeria**   **AWARD** | **Bronze**

Background

How do we capture & amplify the euphoric energy of the World Cup to become the most talked about brand of the 2018 FIFA World Cup in Nigeria in the context of watershed restriction in the category and during the most cluttered period in Nigeria. While also challenging the other global & local sponsors i.e Coca Cola, Hisense, Hyundai for share of presence. Simply put, The world cup presents opportunities for all brands to leverage association with football. In other to succeed within the clutter associated with the world biggest spectacle, we needed to win the attention war by earning our way into the World Cup conversation, not interrupt it. This meant a deep understanding of the media and digital behavior of football fans to provide the right experiences, produce the right content, work with the right partners and distribute content in an effective and timely way.

Strategy

We wanted to work around the media legislation around alcoholic brands in Nigeria, skewing the campaign to the best medium that resonated with our core target market and creatively beating watershed restriction to cut through

Football is a natural passion point for Nigerians, and the FWC gives the brand the opportunity to not only play in the game watching space but capitalize on the euphoric spirit for what happens after the game.

We also realized that the World Cup is not only about the game, it's about the celebrations, the wins, and we called this the light up moments. Instead of focusing on the game like everyone else was, we keyed into these light up moments and built our media strategy and deployment campaign around this.

Execution

we partnered with DSTV, the media broadcast sponsor and locked down Public Viewing centres rights also with Kwese sports to guarantee exclusive broadcast experience.

We kicked off our campaign by lighting up the World Cup in Nigeria with our TVC. We then stirred up massive conversations with a resounding promise: we pledged to give free beer to every Nigerian if the national team gets to the quarterfinals! This was amplified across all key platforms and of course got a lot of media attention. We had a press wrap- around in the most read Newspaper with the caption " Free Bud for every Nigerian"

The conversation was kept going as we asked our twitter fans to show their support for the national team by lighting up their profiles with the Nigerian flag on twitter using conversation cards.

We held light up parties at key viewing centers in Lagos and used celebrities/influencers to drive engagement across the venues on every match day. The "Man Of The Match" trophies were given out at the viewing centers.

Results

Budweiser was the No 1 talked about brand in the category with 64% SOV during the period.

We won the in -bar visiblity at key premium sport bars during the tourmanment.

TV Reach achieved was 86%

GRPS achieved was 1880

Impression = 69m

Video Views= 2.6m

Value = $589m

Earned media = 80%

•Light Up Your Profile was a success as a lot of our audience participated and changed their profile pics as well

•Our partnership with Uber also helped drive conversations during the Final game and free beer given away.

USE OF MEDIA

| Sky Girls Aerogram Competition

CREDITS

Benjamin Anyan - Creative Director
Now Available Africa

Colin Yesutor - Senior Art Director
Now Available Africa

Constance Efua - Junior Art Director
Now Available Africa

Thelma Boama - Copywriter
Now Available Africa

Avevor Events - Co-ordinator
Now Available Africa

Acheampong - Account Manager
Now Available Africa

Deborah Owusua - Account Executive
Now Available Africa

CLIENT I Good Business   **AGENCY I Now Available Africa**   **AWARD I Bronze**

SITUATION

Teenage girls are amongst the hardest audience to engage in Ghana. SKY Girls GH, set up to empower young girls and funded by the Bill & Melinda Gates foundation knows this best. Most of them don't own phones or radios.
BRIEF
How do you have a meaningful two-way conversation with teens who are not 'connected'?
ed refine our messaging and build a stronger relationship with them.

OBJECTIVES

To have the target demonstrate their understanding of the Sky Girls mantra 'Be true to yourself', the sky messaging and the Sky Girls Pledge ('I pledge to be true to myself and what I believe in. To be who I am, not who someone else thinks I should be. I will hold tight to the things I'm all about, like friends and dancing. I will stay away from yawa things I know I'm good without like backstabbing and smoking. Because knowing what my thing and what's not my thing helps make me who I am. I will make choices that are true to me. I pledge to find my sky).

STRATEGY

A campaign built around re-introducing Ghanaian teen girls to the classic communication medium, Letter writing. We place the aerogram into the Sky magazine, we then distributed the magazine in our catchment area and to girls within the target for Sky (13-16 year olds), To make the postal logistics easy we spoke with the Ghana postal service who were only too happy to work with us to allow those entering the competition to send their aerograms to us free of postage charges. We also organized a special bulk letter delivery service directly to our office, so with all the major barriers to entry were removed, all the girls needed to do was put pen to paper, seal and post!

EXECUTION

We created the Sky Aerogram competition! which ran for two months. We put a specially-designed aerogram into the Sky teen-girl themed magazine and distributed 20,000 across our catchment area. With new-media making letter-writing a near-extinct channel, the Ghana Post was excited to partner us, making it free for the girls to write us and simplifying delivery! Each Aerogram could be posted free of any charge to the girls and we organised bulk delivery of the posted letters to our office.
We asked the girls to tear out the aerogram from the magazine and write to us, telling us about their best friends and how they stay true to themselves. It was uncertain if teens - who hardly write letters these days or use the postal system- would write to us at all.

OUTCOME

The response was overwhelming, requiring us to frequently empty our mailbox. We received 4,000 aerogram entries in the competition. Beyond answering our question, girls went on to give personal messages, messages they'll have had no other means to convey. Also Ghana post recorded collecting 60% more letters than they normally collect from the same schools.
After a thorough marking process, the winner was announced at a special event. Their letters gave us deep insights that help.

USE OF INFLUENCERS AND BRAND AMBASSADORS

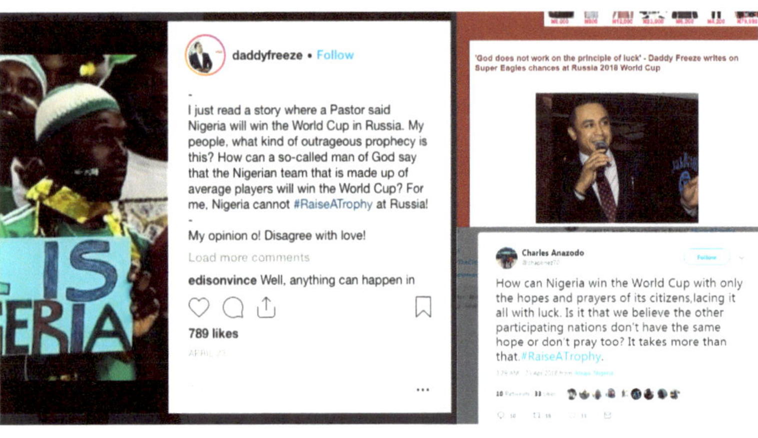

Raise A Trophy

AGENCY | Culture Communications

CLIENT | International Breweries PLC.- ABInBev Family

AWARD | Bronze

Background

Although there is a resurgent belief around the Super Eagles' chances of doing well at the FWC, very few Nigerians have any expectation of Nigeria going far... and with good reason. No African team has ever gotten to the semi-finals of the big stage, let alone win it.

But who says the Super Eagles can't achieve the impossible by going all the way to lift the Trophy? Who says we can't replicate a similar feat of being the first African team to win the football Olympic gold? Who says beating Argentina on a neutral ground was just a fluke that can't be repeated? If Leicester City could achieve the impossible over 38 matches, why can't we do same over 7 matches?

Because Nigerian's pride themselves as people who rise to a challenge, Trophy lager will ignite an unprecedented wave of BELIEF amongst fans in symbolic gesture by holding a Trophy to their chest. Demonstrating belief in the team to rise to each challenge is the HONORABLE thing to do.

Creative Idea

BRAND TRUTH
Trophy exists to accord respect to "Honourable Men"

INSIGHTS

Dishonorable men give up before the game starts, but Honourable men believe their team will rise to the challenge in any engagement.

CULTURAL TRUTH
The true test of patriotism is when fans stand together and believe their team will honour the occasion by rising to the challenge no matter who the opponent
may be.

Strategy

CAMPAIGN/EXECUTION
* Media Campaign breaks across all channels along with the Belief Anthem performed by the artistes.
Anthem permeates radio airplay.
Kick-start #RaiseATrophy Video Challenge.
* Our influencers amplify the launch of the Beliefometer- a digital aggregator interface of all fans that are expressing their belief through #RaiseATrophy- which will be syndicated across popular sites.
* This will culminate in raising the BIGGEST FWC TROPHY using Trophy cans as a monument to the honourable fans that believe. This will also serve to inspire our national team.

Execution

* One hour before every Super Eagles' match, we will have the "Beliefometer Hour" where special rewards will be given to selected fans revving up our Beliefometer. Within the hour, 5 mins before every Nigeria match, a 1-minute extract of the Belief anthem will be played on all major radio stations.
* In the event that the Super Eagles fail to achieve the impossible, we steer our message towards "HONOUR IS NOT IN FAILING, BUT IN FAILING TO TRY".

Results

*An Increment sales of the brand- Trophy Lager.
*Business target was met due to the success of the Campaign.
*The large numbers of people switched to the brand.

INTEGRATED CAMPAIGNS

| SKY GIRLS GH

CLIENT	Good Business
AGENCY	Now Available Africa
AWARD	Gold

CREDITS

Benjamin Anyan - Creative Director
Now Available Africa

Colin Yesutor - Senior Art Director
Now Available Africa

Constance Efua - Junior Art Director
Now Available Africa

Audrey Quaye - Junior Art Director
Now Available Africa

Thelma Boama - Copywriter
Now Available Africa

Whiney Dena Thompson - Community Manager
Now Available Africa

Ernest Kwablah - Community Manager
Now Available Africa

Fuseini Isaac Addo - Production Manager
Now Available Africa

Akwesi Agyekum - Video Editor/ Animator
Now Available Africa

Charles Nunekpeku - Production Assistance
Now Available Africa

Alfred Lebene Avevor - Event Co-ordinator
Now Available Africa

Emeka Precious Dele - Media Strategist
Now Available Africa

George Acheampong - Media Planning Executive
Now Available Africa

Yvonne Acheampong - Account Manager
Now Available Africa

Deborah Owusua Agyena - Account Executive
Now Available Africa

Anna Agostinelli - Project Co-ordinator Magazines
Now Available Africa

Kofi Ocloo Client Service Director
Now Available Africa

Background

Statistics showed that the numbers of youth engaging in tobacco related activities was growing in Ghana especially amongst teenage girls. In a culture where 'smoking' is a taboo subject, the brief was to find a way to engage with teen girls on the subject that would help them develop necessary refusal skills to ward off negative peer influence especially in the area of smoking tobacco. The objectives were to build a movement that would empower teen girls by encouraging them to stay true to themselves, build confidence, follow their passions and strip the aspiration from smoking tobacco.

Creative Idea

SKY GIRLS GH is an anti-tobacco movement with the objective of empowering teen girls by encouraging them to stay true to themselves, build confidence, follow their passions and develop necessary refusal skills to ward off negative peer influence especially in the area of smoking tobacco. Built using a fully integrated approach.

Rather than creating a direct anti-smoking campaign, we elevated the conversation by creating a cool lifestyle platform for teenage girls in Accra. We created a movement that targeted these girls by giving them a platform to feel free and express themselves. We gave them, confidence, a voice and a vehicle through which they can show who they are and in this way, we made them stay true to themselves.

In the messaging, we stay away from direct messaging, like telling the girls not to use tobacco substances but to stick to the things which are positive and to stay away from negative vibes such as gossiping, backbiting, peer pressure before we plug in the smoking.

Strategy

The target for SKY GIRLS GH are teenage girls between the age of 13-17 that live in Accra Ghana.

It is executed on several multimedia platforms, through various activities both digital (Website, Facebook, Instagram, Youtube, WhatsApp) and traditional (including events, activations, Print Magazine, Radio, OOH - Graffiti walls, Billboards, Bus branding, Bus Shelter branding).This integration of touch-points are impacting the lives of young teenage girls in Ghana positively and successfully.

The approach is to engage them in fun loving ways including Online competitions, In-school activations, Radio shows, monthly free magazines with over 20,000 copies distributed per edition, video productions including Weekly Vlogs on YouTube, Movies (Sugar, Spice N Sauce 1&2), clubs in schools, activations in communities and schools where we engage and interact with them.

Although fun in its flavour, at the heart of this campaign, is the objective of stripping the aspiration from smoking tobacco.

Execution

During 2018 to date activities have included online competitions, In-school activations, radio shows, monthly free magazines with a minimum of 20,000 copies distributed per edition, video productions including weekly Vlogs on YouTube, Movies (Sugar, Spice N Sauce 1&2), clubs in schools, and BTL activations in communities and schools. Occasionally, the movement organizes vacation parties that bring over 3000 girls within Accra together. Aside this the girls look forward to receiving a host of Sky branded merchandise including note books, keyrings, base-ball caps, t-shirts, bags, pencils cases, sneakers and stickers.

The movement enjoys the support of The Ghana Education Service and other religious groups which has allowed us smooth entry into both Junior and Senior High schools in Accra. Several influential female personalities with passions for empowering young girls have been involved, MzVee, Kokui Selormey, Adina, YaaYaa, Berla Mundi to name a few.

Results

190,000 Magazines Distributed from April 2017 till date

Over 33,000 girls in Accra signed up to be a part of the movement

Over 100,000 followers across social media (Facebook, WhatsApp, Instagram, YouTube)

Over 700,000 movie views

Visited over 300 schools and over 50 communities in Accra

The movement has contributed significantly in building the confidence of teen girls by providing them the opportunity to take the lead and contribute to meaningful projects and activities like content co-production, emceeing, presenting, writing, acting and mentorship. There has been significant decrease in the positive perception of Shisha amongst the youth especially teen girls.

INTEGRATED CAMPAIGNS

CREDITS

Augustine Efienamokwu -
Business Head/Media Director
Vizeum Nigeria

Ola Olowo - CCO/MD
Isobar

Oluwatobi Alabi - Digital Manager
Iprospect

Joshua Oyeleye - Media Strategy Manager
Vizeum

Budweiser FIFA WORLD CUP

CLIENT | **ABInBev** **AGENCY** | **Vizeum Nigeria** **AWARD** | **Silver**

Background

How do we capture & amplify the euphoric energy of the World Cup to become the most talked about brand of the 2018 FIFA World Cup in Nigeria in the context of watershed restriction in the category and during the most cluttered period in Nigeria. While also challenging the other global & local sponsors i.e Coca Cola, Hisense, Hyundai for share of presence. Simply put, The world cup presents opportunities for all brands to leverage association with football. In other to succeed within the clutter associated with the world biggest spectacle, we needed to win the attention war by earning our way into the World Cup conversation, not interrupt it. This meant a deep understanding of the media and digital behavior of football fans to provide the right experiences, produce the right content, work with the right partners and distribute content in an effective and timely way.

Strategy

We wanted to work around the media legislation around alcoholic brands in Nigeria, skewing the campaign to the best medium that resonated with our core target market and creatively beating watershed restriction to cut through

Football is a natural passion point for Nigerians, and the FWC gives the brand the opportunity to not only play in the game watching space but capitalize on the euphoric spirit for what happens after the game.

We also realized that the World Cup is not only about the game, it's about the celebrations, the wins, and we called this the light up moments. Instead of focusing on the game like everyone else was, we keyed into these light up moments and built our media strategy and deployment campaign around this.

Execution

we partnered with DSTV, the media broadcast sponsor and locked down Public Viewing centres rights also with Kwese sports to guarantee exclusive broadcast experience.

We kicked off our campaign by lighting up the World Cup in Nigeria with our TVC. We then stirred up massive conversations with a resounding promise: we pledged to give free beer to every Nigerian if the national team gets to the quarterfinals! This was amplified across all key platforms and of course got a lot of media attention. We had a press wrap- around in the most read Newspaper with the caption " Free Bud for every Nigerian"

The conversation was kept going as we asked our twitter fans to show their support for the national team by lighting up their profiles with the Nigerian flag on twitter using conversation cards.

We held light up parties at key viewing centers in Lagos and used celebrities/influencers to drive engagement across the venues on every match day. The "Man Of The Match" trophies were given out at the viewing centers.

Results

Budweiser was the No 1 talked about brand in the category with 64% SOV during the period.

We won the in -bar visiblity at key premium sport bars during the tourmanment.

TV Reach achieved was 86%

GRPS achieved was 1880

Impression = 69m

Video Views= 2.6m

Value =$589m

Earned media = 80%

•Light Up Your Profile was a success as a lot of our audience participated and changed their profile pics as well

•Our partnership with Uber also helped drive conversations during the Final game and free beer given away.

▌ Enabling Success | Don't be an Uncle Thomas

CLIENT ▍ **Union Bank PLC**   **AGENCY** ▍ **Image and Time**   **AWARD** ▍ **Bronze**

CREDITS

Ogochukwu Ekezie-Ekaidem
Head, Corporate Communications and Marketing
Union Bank of Nigeria

Ngozi Akinyele - Head Strategic Brand Management,
Corporate Communication & Marketing
Union Bank of Nigeria

Akorede Zakaraya - Creative Director
Image & Time

Chris Dada - Director
Image & Time

Bukola Akingbade - Managing Partner
Neukleos

Jade James-Omitiran - Account Director
Image & Time

Michael Adediji - Assitant Creative Director
Image & Time

Tolani Olusoga - Account Manager
Image & Time

Background

The Union Bank brand has evolved significantly in its over 100 years of existence. In the last 6 years, we transformed their business model, people, systems, completely re-positioning our brand from the big, strong, reliable bank to your simpler, smarter bank.

Coming off our centenary celebration, the brand announced our commitment to partner for the country's development over the next 100 years, we needed to establish ourselves as a trusted financial partner and a success enabler for the society while shaking of the perception of being an old and archaic bank.

Creative Idea

ENABLING SUCCESS (DON'T BE AN UNCLE THOMAS)

We presented ourselves as success enablers. We help you reach your dreams, provided you do not let wrong perceptions, doubt or pessimism get in the way.

To show this, we created a scapegoat called Uncle Thomas, to show how doubt and pessimism can get in the way of success.

We presented doubting "Uncle Thomas" and his mindset as the person you should not be and the mindset you should not have.

The idea being that while doubt and cynicism are sometimes legitimate emotions in a challenging nation like Nigeria, we still should not give in to pessimism and apathy

Strategy

We stayed true to our commitment to enable the success of everyday Nigerians by executing a fully Nigerian advert. In a timely move, we launched the Enabling Success campaign on Independence Day, leading up to a pivotal election in the country.

The TVC received critical acclaim and currently has over a million views on YouTube (The highest number of views a Nigerian ad has ever had on the platform). The ads also ran on other platforms such as radio, OOH; LED screens, static billboards, wall drapes and lampposts.

Execution

We stayed true to our commitment to enable the success of everyday Nigerians by executing a fully Nigerian advert. In a timely move, we launched the Enabling Success campaign on Independence Day, leading up to a pivotal election in the country.

The TVC received critical acclaim and currently has over a million views on YouTube.

Results

Brand equity increased by 14.9%

Net Promoter Score increased by 32%

Uncle Thomas became a lingo in pop-culture.

The ad triggered social conversations

The video had approx. 4 million views across all digital platforms within 4 weeks, and remains the Nigerian ad with the highest number of YouTube views till date

20% increase in new accounts opening

90% increase in reactivated bank accounts

Yielded 95% of the target gross rating points across radio, TV and OOH

INTEGRATED CAMPAIGNS

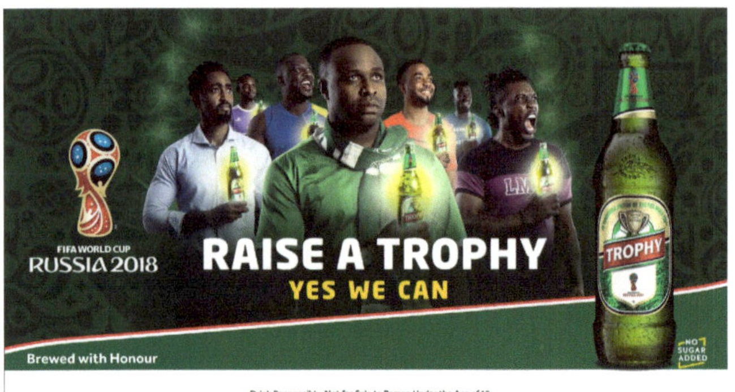

Raise A Trophy

CLIENT | International Breweries PLC. (ABInBev Nigeria)

AGENCY | Culture Communications

AWARD | Bronze

Background

The Brief

To grow brand relevance and engagement amongst consumers by leveraging the brand rights to the 2018 FIFA World Cup assets to create a compelling 360 degree communications campaign.

Creative Idea

Raise A Trophy

Although there is a resurgent belief around the Super Eagles' chances of doing well at the FIFA WORLD CUP, very few Nigerians have any expectation of Nigeria going far... and with good reason- No African team has ever gotten to the semi-finals of the big stage, let alone win it.

But who says the Super Eagles can't achieve the impossible by going all the way to lift the Trophy? Who says we can't replicate a similar feat of being the first African team to win the football Olympic gold? Who says beating Argentina on a neutral ground was just a fluke that can't be repeated? If Leicester City could achieve the impossible over 38 matches, why can't we do same over 7 matches?

Because Nigerian's pride themselves as people who rise to a challenge. Trophy lager will ignite an unprecedented wave of BELIEF amongst fans in symbolic gesture by holding a Trophy to their chest. Demonstrating belief in the team to rise to each challenge is the HONORABLE thing to do.

Strategy

RAISE A TROPHY

Brand Truth: Trophy exists to accord respect to "Honourable Men".

Insights: Dishonorable men give up before the game starts, but Honourable men believe their team will rise to the challenge in any engagement.

Cultural Truth: The true test of patriotism is when fans stand

together and believe their team will honour the occasion by rising to the challenge no matter who the opponent may be.

Execution

CAMPAIGN / EXECUTION

PRE-CAMPAIGN Teaser Buzz:

1. Popular on-air personalities and social media influencers kick-start debate on the possibility of Nigeria going all the way. The debate coalesces around the hashtag #YesWeCan.

2. Trophy Lager weighs into the conversations with the hashtag #RaiseATrophy #YesWeCan, amplified by influencers and our selected popular music artistes.

3. The debate trickles into other media channels: live radio debates, blogsites, newspapers, online polls.

CAMPAIGN Launch:

4. Media Campaign breaks across all channels along with the Belief Anthem performed by the artistes.

Anthem permeates radio airplay.

Kick-start #RaiseATrophy Video Challenge

5. Our influencers amplify the launch of the Beliefometer- a digital aggregator interface of all fans that are expressing their belief through #RaiseATrophy- which will be syndicated across popular sites.

6. This will culminate in raising the BIGGEST FWC TROPHY using Trophy cans as a monument to the honourable fans

Results

Business Results: Rapid growth in sales and marketing. The Campaign increases sales of the brand all over above stipulated regions.

It drives more traffic to the website, facebook, Instagram and Twitter through Brand Ambassadors and Brand Influencers.

CREDITS

Yomi Benson - Managing Director
Culture Communications

Akin Akingbola - Creative Director
Culture Communications

Samuel Olonisakin - Art Director
Culture Communications

Nathaniel Ogbu - Account Manager
Culture Communications

Clem Onah- Elebuwa - Copywriter
Culture Communications

Dare Okuntilu - Head, Client Service
Culture Communications

Olufunke Fajusigbe - Photographer
Auxilia Images Concept

INTEGRATED CAMPAIGNS

CLIENT | **Seven-Up Bottling Company/PepsiCo International**
AGENCY | **All Seasons Zenith**
AWARD | **Bronze**

Pepsi Naija All The Way Campaign (World Cup 2018)

Background

Pepsi in trying to own the hearts and minds of the Nigerian youth consumers has always focused on their two biggest passion points; Music & Football. The World Cup, being the biggest football event in the world presents a huge opportunity for the brand to excite and engage her target audience, etching her mark in their minds.

However, Coca-Cola, the ancient rival of Pepsi played a fast one by obtaining sponsorship rights to the World Cup. This means that Pepsi as well as other competing brands have no rights to use any World Cup property in communication and branding. This limited Pepsi a great deal in what she could do to leverage on this great event to achieve her objective of exciting and engaging her fans but, the brand creatively outsmarted her competition in achieving them.

Creative Idea

Since the brand had no right to any World Cup property, having been obtained by Coca-Cola, the brand leveraged on the emotion and pride of the Nigerian football fans of their root and spirit in creating excitement and buzz. This birthed the "Naija All The Way" mantra which celebrates the Nigerian resilient, "Can Do" and positivity spirit.

We used Pepsi's Football ambassadors to emphasize the brand's support of the Nigerian national team at the World Cup; the music and DJ ambassadors to generate excitement and sense of pride in the Naija pop culture and a Legendary ambassador (J.J. Okocha) to build nostalgia and relive Nigeria's glory years at past World Cup competitions.

Strategy

Pepsi's target audience, primarily youths between 16 and 24 years (C1C2DE, SEC) are mobile and dynamic, hence our strategy was digital-led 360 degree communication strategy.

On digital, we deployed our communication on Goal.com, popular blogs, Youtube and we used influencers to engage our TG.

The communication was amplified offline on Radio (spots, hypes and time checks), TV (spots on terrestrial and cable TV stations and on live matches), Print and BRT.

On Radio, we deployed 60 secs & 45 secs jingles on top rated stations and sports programmes for high reach and high frequency; hypes to create excitement among our target audience; and time checks for momentary disruption.

On TV, we had placements on live matches and we deployed on rated terrestrial and cable TV channels and programmes that resonate with our TG.

We had placements on top-rated print vehicles, especially Complete Sports leveraging on their popularity for World Cup news and updates.

We used BRT for inner-city penetration.

Execution

The campaign kicked off with the reveal of the TVC on Pepsi's social media pages and on some rated terrestrial and cable TV channels a week before the World Cup kick-off. The brand's influencers amplified the TVC on their pages to generate buzz and trend for #NaijaAllTheWay.

Communications on Radio, Print & BRT were deployed two days after the reveal and continued until the National Team crashed out of the competition.

The radio jingles and TVCs were scheduled in a way that placements were increased on Nigeria match days and the day before the match days, to arouse emotion and support for the team. Radio hypes ran for four days and time checks ran until Nigeria exited. For print, we had insertions on the match days and the day after the match days. BRT deployment was for the entire duration of the World Cup.

Although we stopped all communications including digital upon Nigeria's exit from the competition, our communication in live matches continued till the end of the competition.

Results

Milestone achieved by the campaign are;
Twitter: 672,564,243 Twitter timeline impressions, reaching 138,090,346 unique Twitter users, contributed by a total of 55,223 Twitter users. Pepsi's followers increased from 110,900 to 136,386; gaining 25,486 new followers.

Instagram: 170,362,826 #NaijaAllTheWay impressions reaching 64,841,255 unique Instagram users. Pepsi's followers increased from 96,300 to 110,501; gaining 14,201 new followers.

Facebook: Pepsi's followers increased from 1,102,215 to 1,111,814; gaining 9,629 new followers.

CREDITS

Cynthia Ogbonna - Group Head, Strategy & Planning
All Seasons Zenith

Adewunmi Ebuku - Deputy Manager, Strategy & Planning
All Seasons Zenith

Oluwaseun Sanni - Deputy Manager, Strategy & Planning
All Seasons Zenith

PR AND REPUTATION MANAGEMENT

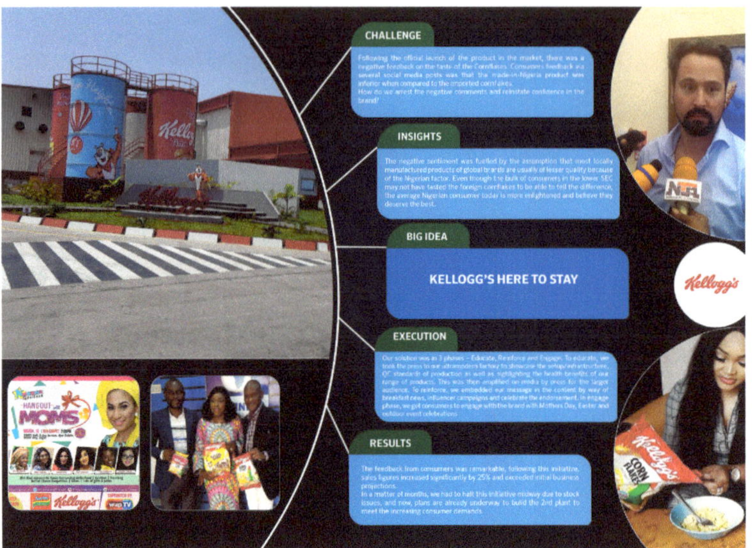

Kellogg's Here to Stay

CREDITS

Yinka Adebayo ED - Media Investment
OMD

Mariam Kuku - Planner
OMD

Folahan Oluladem - Planner
OMD

CLIENT **|** **Kellogg Tolaram**   AGENCY **|** **mediaReachOMD**   AWARD **|** **Gold**

Background

Following the official launch of the Kellogg's brand in the Nigerian Market, there was negative feedback on the taste of the cornflakes. Consumer feedback via several social media post was that the now made in Nigeria product was inferior when compared to the imported cornflakes. This was going to impact on the perception of the consumer and also possibly impact on the confidence associated with the product offering and quality associated with the company

Creative Idea

In tackling this critical issue, we had a deep dive to clearly understand the key insights and can be unraveled to unearth a solution. We discovered that the negative sentiment was fueled by the assumption that most locally manufactured products of global brands are usually of lesser quality because of the "Nigerian Factor". even though the bulk of the consumers in the lower SEC may not have tasted the foreign cornflakes to be able to tell the difference, the average Nigerian consumer today is more enlightened and believe they deserve the best. We decided to imprint the core of quality to express confidence across key execution by expressing the fact that Kellogg's Here to Stay and it is of the same global quality

Strategy

Our Core Strategy was to Educate- for consumers to appreciate the core essence of the brand and the processes involved in production for them to know that quality standards involved in the process. We also seek to Reinforce the position of the brand within the category to enhance confidence with the consumer. And we seek to Engage so we can possibly drive the conversation further and make our consumers advocates.

Execution

Our execution was in the three strategic layers: Educate, Reinforce and Engage. To Educate, we took the press to our ultramodern factory to showcase the setup/infracstructure, Quality Control standards of production as well as highlithing the health benefits of our range of products. This was then amplified on media by press for the larger audience. To Reinforce, we embedded our message in the content by way of breakfast news, influencers campaign and celebrated the endorsement . To Engage, we got consumers to celebrate with Kellogs leveraging key occasions like Mothers Day, Easter and Outdoor event celebrations

Results

The positive feedback from the consumers were remarkable. Following the executions/initiative, sales figures increased significantly by 25% and exceeded initial business projections. In months, we had to halt this initiative due to stock issues as supply could not meet demand. Plans are currently underway to build the 2nd plant to meet the increasing consumer demands

PR AND REPUTATION MANAGEMENT

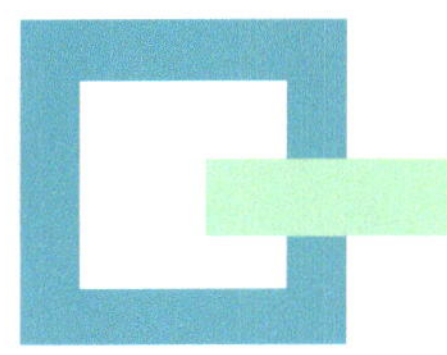

CREDITS

Henry Eguridu - Senior Consultant
Chain Reactions Nigeria

Uchechi Onuoha - Senior Analyst
Chain Reactions Nigeria

Lere Ojedokun
Executive Director, Strategic Communications
Chain Reactions Nigeria

| Polaris Bank

CLIENT	**Polaris Bank**	AGENCY	**Chain Reactions**	AWARD	**Silver**

Background

The Central Bank of Nigeria, on Friday, September 21, 2018, revoked the operating license of Skye Bank PLC. In its place, Central Bank established a bridge bank, Polaris Bank Limited, which took over all assets and liabilities (including staff and customers plus their accounts and records) of the defunct entity. Governor of the CBN, Godwin Emefiele, who made the shocking announcement at a media conference in Lagos, stated further that the Nigeria Deposit Insurance Corporation (NDIC) had sold the new entity Polaris Bank to Asset Management Corporation of Nigeria (AMCON) to ensure stability and profitability of the new entity preparatory to future sale to interested investors in 2023, its sunset year, otherwise ownership will revert to CBN and the Federal Ministry of Finance, who co-own AMCON.

Creative Idea

Our strategy was "COMMUNICATIONS WAR ROOM", which is a Creative Newsroom Model or what is commonly called 'The Situation Room'.

We worked with Polaris Bank's strategic brand management and corporate communications team to proactively plan communications which included development of Key Messages, Story Bank and Content Calendar for strategic deployment

Creatively and credibly respond to all offline and online negative views and opinions expressed about the bank and developed unique angles and content to opportunistically pitch Polaris Bank stories

Repurpose existing content for opportunistic play

Uncover new opportunities for spokespersons and influencers

Strategy

Our Strategy was tagged "Build The Knowledge Bridge" and provided a connect between,

THE PRESENT
* Transition Brand
* Uncertainty among Customers
* Uncertainty among Shareholders
* Government Backing
* Low Perception

THE VEHICLE
Build the Knowledge Bridge

THE DESTINATION
* Business Stability
* Customer Retention & Brand Loyalty
* Empathy & Understanding
* Gain Brand equity
* Improved Positive Perception

Execution

Behind-The-Scene Engagements and Alignments
Pre-emptive Decapitation of Issues and Rebuttals
Precedent Communication
Expert Opinion Marketing and Endorsement
Credible Communications

Results

Through our Communication War Room strategy, we executed PR Communication and Reputation Management that ensured we decapitated false news and negative sentiments about the new Polaris Bank and its Management.

We deepened the understanding of critical stakeholders about the CBN intervention by equipping them with adequate information and facts; allayed fear of critical stakeholders such as customers of the safety of their deposits through reinforcement of assurances by credible authorities/testimonials, and positively positioned Polaris Bank as a reliable and trustworthy bank with a sound future.

PR AND REPUTATION MANAGEMENT

CLIENT	I	**X3M IDEAS**
AGENCY	I	**X3M IDEAS**
AWARD	I	**Bronze**

Shapeshifters Campaign

CREDITS

Steve Babaeko - Chief Creative Officer
X3M IDEAS

Adesola Akosoko - Creative Director
X3M IDEAS

Godwin Ndubuisi - Deputy Creative Director
X3M IDEAS

Femi Akowonjo - Senior Copywriter
X3M IDEAS

Kelechi Uduma - Copywriter
X3M IDEAS

Simi Ajayi - Copywriter
X3M IDEAS

Saturday Emmanuel - Motion Graphic Artist
X3M IDEAS

Israel Obatunde - Art Director
X3M IDEAS

Kimson Masters - Illustrator
X3M IDEAS

Background

In today's world, brands are competing for the same clients both local and global. However, the clients' budgets are not necessarily getting any bigger, making the competition even tougher. So how do you stay visible and relevant?

Creative Idea

To express this very important business mantra as the soul of X3M Ideas, the agency launched a new philosophy; SHAPESHIFTERS.

Strategy

To express this very important business mantra as the soul of X3M Ideas, the agency launched a new philosophy; SHAPESHIFTERS.

Describe the Execution

We buried fake dinosaur fossil and used influencers to start the conversation. This generated a wide-spread conversation about the dinosaur.

Results

22million impressions and 13million reach on twitter.

Also got over 400,000 impressions and over 300,000 reach on instagram.

It eventually got carried by several news platforms including ChannelsTV, Nigeria's No 1 news platform.

We got positive response from the public including business owners and get to emphasize the need to ADAPT or DIE.

PR AND REPUTATION MANAGEMENT

Food Fest

CREDITS

Ajibike Onabadejo - Content
digitXplus

CLIENT | **UAC Restautant**   **AGENCY** | **digitXplus**   **AWARD** | **Bronze**

Background

Mr Biggs being one of the longest restaurant chains in Nigeria overtime, had dropped in quality of food, overall customer experience, sales and brand affinity; This was negatively affecting the brands perception.

With about 35 outlets spread across Lagos; the modern audience weren't resonating with the brand

We needed to show the brand as one willing to evolve with their offerings in order to meet and exceed existing and potential customers' needs and create a watering hole to pull of the modern audience into the restaurants.

Creative Idea

The modern audience had needs that had evolved with time; With a lot more restaurants springing up and evolving in the meal offerings the target audience had a lot more options of where they could dine; and variety was one of the key considerations.

They will only be loyal to a brand that offered great quality and variety at the best possible price in a great ambience- Seeing is believing.

Strategy

We used a celebrity chef to develop a new menu to attract the modern audience and to leverage on a 2 day food festival to bring both new and potential customers together to have fun whilst sampling some of the new meals being introduced by the restaurant.

Execution

We developed a Microsite for people to register for the event and ran an extensive marketing campaign to create awareness of the upcoming event by leveraging on the emotional currency of the TA connecting with their Mr Biggs experience of old times with conversation triggers like " Its time to switch up our recipes up a notch"

3 food bloggers and 2 PR influencers created hypes and awareness about the upcoming event to generate talkability.

On the event days, we created experiences at the Food Fest to get people to constantly remember the event as a memorable one by Live streaming the event online and a photo booth to provide picture props and capture memories of the guests that came for the event.

Results

We were able to overcome the primary challenge of getting footfalls which we achieved with the Food fest with over 5,000 people registering as against the planned 2000 which was over 150% above the set target and the turn up at the event for both days was also massive and much beyond expectation.

Secondly with a large variety of over 30 different meals at an affordable price; , we were able to cater to the needs of the people that turned up for the Food fest showcasing the new menu.

SOCIAL MEDIA CAMPAIGN

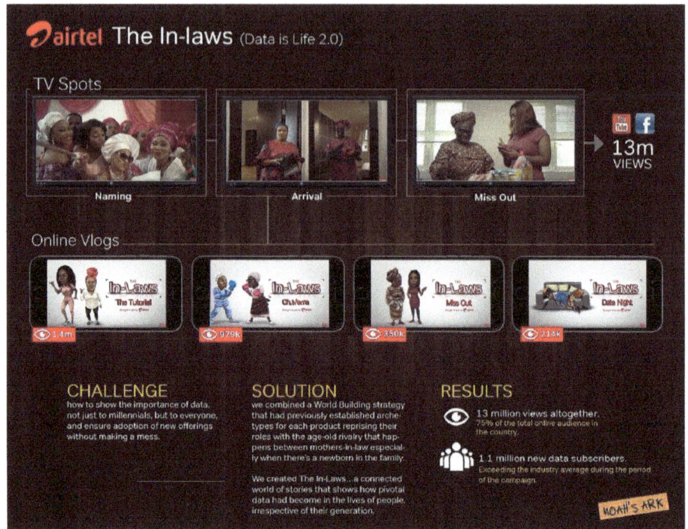

In-laws

CREDITS

Lanre Adisa - Chief Creative Officer
Noah's Ark Communications

Eyo Ekeno - Chief Operating Officer
Noah's Ark Communications

Abolaji Alausa - Executive Creative Director
Noah's Ark Communications

Maurice Ugwonoh - Creative Director
Noah's Ark Communications

Solomon Osafile - Deputy Creative Director
Noah's Ark Communications

Baruch Apata - Copywiter
Noah's Ark Communications

Ezekiel Resedenz - Art Director
Noah's Ark Communications

Mitch Defounga - Art Director
Noah's Ark Communications

CLIENT | Airtel

AGENCY | Noah's Ark Communications

AWARD | Gold

Background

Beyond being a "youth thing", data had become a lot more mainstream in Nigeria, with Facebook itself saying it had over one million Nigerians over the age of 60 accessing its platform. With more data products in its kitty, Airtel needed to communicate to larger audience.

Creative Idea

We developed "The In-laws" a series of short stories that demonstrated the need for data across generations, by using a series of video content to show how important data has become to both the digital natives as well as older generations.

Strategy

We adopted a "world building" strategy of getting characters in previous Airtel ads to reprise their other roles within one universe, and hinged it on the the age long rivalry between mother in laws in the Nigerian society.

Execution

What better way to sell data, than to use a medium that is native to it? We used a series of online films, and video logs, following the lives of the various characters, and showing how data played a role in it. We also supported the campaign with caricature digital banners that brought the characters to life even more.

Results

Online videos were positively received, getting 13m views across Facebook and Youtube

Watch time for vlogs exceeded the industry average for videos over a minute, and gathered views, Tutorial-1.4m, Oh Mama-979k, Miss Out-350k, and Date Night-214k

Campaign reached an estimated 75% of the digital audience in Nigeria

Airtel added 1.1m new data subscribers, the quarter after the campaign ran, according to stats from NCC.

The brand exceeded the industry average for subscriber growth, and surged to become the fastest growing telecom brand in Nigeria.

SOCIAL MEDIA CAMPAIGN

| Work Out with Whatever

CLIENT	**Three Crowns**
AGENCY	**Noah's Ark Communications**
AWARD	**Bronze**

CREDITS

Lanre Adisa - Chief Creative Officer
Noah's Ark Communications

Eyo Ekeno - Chief Operating Officer
Noah's Ark Communications

Abolaji Alausa - Executive Creative Director
Noah's Ark Communications

Maurice Ugwonoh - Creative Director
Noah's Ark Communications

Yemi Arawore - Creative Director
Noah's Ark Communications

Solomon Osafile - Deputy Creative Director
Noah's Ark Communications

OlaDunni Wonuola - Copywriter
Noah's Ark Communications

Kachee Sera - Copywriter
Noah's Ark Communications

Background

Three Crowns Milk needed to drive up participation for its brand activations platform, the 30 days fitness challenge and the challenge was to develop online content that can drive up participation for the upcoming season.

Creative Idea

We encouraged people to work out with "whatever", by showing how basic household items can be used to work out.

Strategy

Our post campaign evaluation of previous seasons showed that people sometimes restrained from working out because they felt they did not have the right work out gear. We flipped this on its head and made it the core of our campaign.

Execution

Using an online film and digital creatives, we demonstrated the core idea, and also drove traffic to the registration website. We also utilized radio hypes as support and found a way to demonstrate that working out was not just for a select few who had the right equipment.

Results

Over 100,000 views, 15,000 likes and over 3,000 shares on Facebook within a week

10m impressions across Twitter and Instagram

#WorkOutWithWhatever trended three days after on Twitter

Campaign drove up participation beyond Lagos, and the brand expanded its reach to Ibadan and Uyo.

| Ewa Agoyin

CLIENT	**|**	**Hypo**
AGENCY	**|**	**Noah's Ark Communications**
AWARD	**|**	**Gold**

CREDITS

Lanre Adisa - Chief Creative Officer
Noah's Ark Communications

Eyo Ekeno - Chief Operating Officer
Noah's Ark Communications

Abolaji Alausa - Executive Creative Director
Noah's Ark Communications

Maurice Ugwonoh - Creative Director
Noah's Ark Communications

Yemi AraoworeCreative Director
Noah's Ark Communications

Gabriel OlonisakinArt Director
Noah's Ark Communications

Aladeniji Olumaiye - Art Director
Noah's Ark Communications

Sodiq Sheu - Art Director
Noah's Ark Communications

Baruch Apata - Copywriter
Noah's Ark Communications

Kunle Omopo - Copywriter
Noah's Ark Communications

Onyekachi Uju Sarah - Copywriter
Noah's Ark Communications

Mayokun Ajayeoba = Copywriter
Noah's Ark Communications

Maria Omole - Account Manager
Noah's Ark Communications

Yomi Alake - Digital Executive
Noah's Ark Communications

PRINT

CLIENT | Indomie
AGENCY | Noah's Ark
AWARD | Silver

| **Feed Their Imagination**

CREDITS

Lanre Adisa - Chief Creative Officer
Noah's Ark Communications

Eyo Ekeno - Chief Operating Officer
Noah's Ark Communications

Abolaji Alausa - Executive Creative Director
Noah's Ark Communications

Maurice Ugwonoh - Creative Director
Noah's Ark Communications

Solomon Osafile - Deputy Creative Director
Noah's Ark Communications

Kunle Omope - Copywriter
Noah's Ark Communications

Uju Onyekachi - Copywriter
Noah's Ark Communications

Sodiq Sheu - Art Director
Noah's Ark Communications

John Adesanya - Illustrator
Noah's Ark Communications

Olumaiye Aladeniji - 3D Artist
Noah's Ark Communications

| Ramadan

CLIENT **| Indomie Nigeria**　　　AGENCY **| Noah's Ark Communications**　　　AWARD **| Bronze**

CREDITS

Lanre Adisa - Chief Creative Officer
Noah's Ark Communications

Eyo Ekeno - Chief Operating Officer
Noah's Ark Communications

Abolaji Alausa - Executive Creative Director
Noah's Ark Communications

Maurice Ugwonoh - Creative Director
Noah's Ark Communications

Sodiq Sheu - Art Director
Noah's Ark Communications

Kunle Omope - Copywriter
Noah's Ark Communications

Sera Onyekachi - Copywriter
Noah's Ark Communications

John - Illustrator
Noah's Ark Communications

PRINT

CLIENT	Access Bank PLC
AGENCY	Imaginarium Marketing
AWARD	Bronze

Payday Loan Introductory Ad

CREDITS

Olayiwola Akerele - Art Director
Imaginarium Marketing Communication

Samson James - Art Director
Imaginarium Marketing Communication

Emeka Otoba - Copywriter
Imaginarium Marketing Communication

Amyn Bawa-Allah - Copywriter
Imaginarium Marketing Communication

Nkem Monye - Client Services
Imaginarium Marketing Communication

Chukwuemeka Jay - Executive Creative Director
Imaginarium Marketing Communication

Toyin Henry-Ajayi - Head, Advertising
Access Bank PLC

CLIENT		DSTV
AGENCY		X3M Ideas
AWARD		Bronze

DSTV Egg

CREDITS

Femi Bonojo - Art Director

X3M IDEAS

Simi Ajayi - Copywriter

X3M IDEAS

AUDIO

❙ Twinkle Twinkle Little Star

Twinkle -Twinkle Little Star

(to the tune of twinkle-twinkle little star)

LITTLE GIRL: Twinkle, twinkle, little star

I can see my daddy's car

Now he's hurting her again

Mommy's crying out in pain

Twinkle,   twinkle little star

I hate

what he

does to her.

ANNCR: Domestic violence doesn't just hurt adults – it damages children. Help us break the cycle – visit www.projectalertnig.org today.

CLIENT   ❙   **Project Alert NG**   AGENCY   ❙   **Up In The Sky**   AWARD   ❙   **Gold**

CREDITS

Oje Ojeaga - Copywriter
Up In The Sky

Bolanle Akintomide - Producer
Up In The Sky

Omaga Idirigbe - Head, Creative
Up In The Sky

AUDIO

Baa Baa Black Sheep

Baa-Baa Black Sheep

(To the tune of baa baa black sheep)

LITTLE BOY: Baa Baa Black Sheep

have you heard the news?

Yes sir, yes sir, they said abuse!

One stab in his heart,

And one in his brain,

Mommy's now a murderer

(pause)

And I live with the shame.

ANNCR: Women are not the only victims of domestic violence. Help us break the cycle – visit www.projectalertnig.org today.

CLIENT | Project Alert NG
AGENCY | Up In The Sky
AWARD | Silver

CREDITS

Oje Ojeaga - Copywriter
Up In The Sky

Bolanle Akintomide - Producer
Up In The Sky

Omaga Idirigbe - Head, Creative
Up In The Sky

AUDIO

Ramadan

Ustaz: Islamic Cleric

Young Reciter: 10yr old Arabic student who doubles as the one who echoes the Ustaz's words

SFX: Mosque ambience. Indomie Ramadan Music plays in the background

Ustaz: As we all go home

Young Reciter: Ustaz says as we all go home to break

Ustaz: Remember Ramadan is about sharing

Young Reciter: Ramadan is about sharing

Ustaz: So, we can share our fruits

Young Reciter: We can share our fruits

Ustaz: We can share our tea

Young Reciter: We can share our tea

Ustaz: We can even share our Indomie noodles…

Young Reciter: (pause) erm, erm

Ustaz(repeats again): …I say we can share our Indomie noodles

Young Reciter: erm, erm, Ustaz say you can share your own Indomie noodles

Anncr: It's okay to share what you love. Ramadan Kareem.

Ustaz: Malik, where is the Indomie noodles Hajia brought for me?

Young Reciter: We have shared it…

Ustaz: Ahn?!

Payoff: Indomie Noodles..Tasty Nutrition Good For You

CLIENT | **Indomie**   AGENCY | **Noah's Ark Communications**   AWARD | **Bronze**

CREDITS

Lanre Adisa - Chief Creative Officer
Noah's Ark Communications

Eyo Ekeno - Chief Operating Officer
Noah's Ark Communications

Abolaji Alausa - Executive Creative Director
Noah's Ark Communications

Maurice Ugwonoh - Creative Director
Noah's Ark Communications

Funsho Adebayo - Producer
Noah's Ark Communications

Kunle Omope - Copywriter
Noah's Ark Communications

Zainab Giwa - Copywriter
Noah's Ark Communications

Case Study: Ambient OOH- MTN Enterprise Business Unit – MAN IN THE BOX

THE CHALLENGE

Generate awareness for MTN Nigeria Enterprise Business solutions & get the market to know that MTN is more than the consumer solutions offered – Voice and Data
Demonstrate to the SME community that MTN understands what they need to stay in business

THE INSIGHT

SMEs in Nigeria struggle with access to funds, power and competition with imported products. As a result of the cost of operations in Nigeria, many lack or do not consider basic IT infrastructures that could improve their service offerings

THE IDEA

An Outdoor idea to demonstrate the commitment of the brand at delivering telecoms technological based solutions to SMEs. The campaign idea was to create an installation with a man working inside.
This man portrays the brand's commitment to going the extra mile and 'being up at odd hours' to ensure the successes of businesses through telecoms driven solutions

THE EXECUTION

An elevated portal cabin was reconstructed to simulate a billboard with 2 LED screens and an office space.
The LED screens ran a 3day countdown to the unveiling of the man in the box campaign. We had the man in the box tease for 3days, unveiled MTN Enterprise business on the 4th day and for the remaining 5 weeks had SME businesses offer to display their goods in the cabin and run free advert.

THE RESULTS

Reach over 20million Nigerians, drove record level applications to MTN EBU online portal for partnership. The EBU team was awarded the Best Enterprise Business Team across the MTN Group. We also achieved over N50m worth of earned media via news broadcasts, Social media posts, radio and print campaigns.

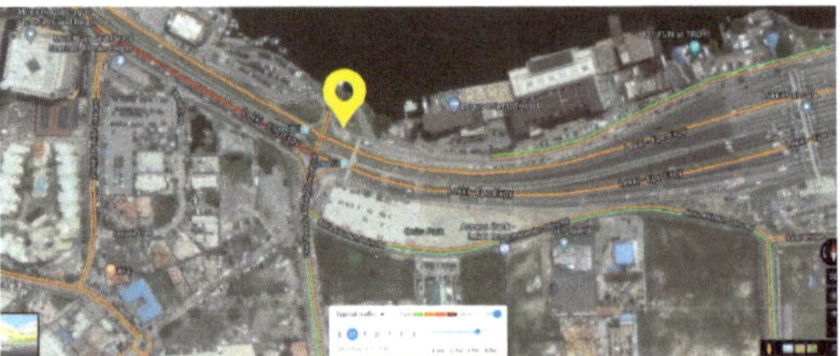

Ambient OOH - Man in the Box

CLIENT	MTN
AGENCY	PHD Nigeria
AWARD	Gold

CREDITS

Victor Oyarero - Team/Project lead
PHD Nigeria

Tope Sanni-Wahab - Project Supervisor
PHD Nigeria

CLIENT | Peak Masterbrand

AGENCY | Noah's Ark Communications Limited

AWARD | Gold

| Let Them Reach Their Peak - Pilot

CREDITS

Lanre Adisa - Chief Creative Officer
Noah's Ark Communications

Eyo Ekeno - Chief Operating Officer
Noah's Ark Communications

Abolaji Alausa - Executive Creative Director
Noah's Ark Communications

Maurice Ugwonoh - Creative Director
Noah's Ark Communications

Gabriel Olonisakin - Art Director
Noah's Ark Communications

Kayode Onimole - Art Director
Noah's Ark Communications

Sodiq Sheu - Art Director
Noah's Ark Communications

Aishat Ademigbuji - Copywriter
Noah's Ark Communications

Seye Kehinde - Photographer
Noah's Ark Communications

Yemi Arawore - Creative Director
Noah's Ark Communications

Solomon Osafile - Deputy Creative Director
Noah's Ark Communications

| Cap

CLIENT | **Airtel**

AGENCY | **Noah's Ark Communications**

AWARD | **Silver**

CREDITS

Lanre Adisa - Chief Creative Officer
Noah's Ark Communications

Eyo Ekeno - Chief Operating Officer
Noah's Ark Communications

Abolaji Alausa - Executive Creative Director
Noah's Ark Communications

Maurice Ugwonoh - Creative Director
Noah's Ark Communications

Solomon Osafile - Deputy Creative Director
Noah's Ark Communications

Baruch Apata - Copywriter
Noah's Ark Communications

Mitch Defounga - Art Director
Noah's Ark Communications

Ezekiel Resedenz - Art Director
Noah's Ark Communications

4G

CLIENT | Airtel   AGENCY | Noah's Ark Communications   AWARD | Bronze

CREDITS

Lanre Adisa - Chief Creative Officer
Noah's Ark Communications

Eyo Ekeno - Chief Operating Officer
Noah's Ark Communications

Abolaji Alausa - Executive Creative Director
Noah's Ark Communications

Maurice Ugwonoh - Creative Director
Noah's Ark Communications

Solomon Osafile - Deputy Creative Director
Noah's Ark Communications

Baruch Apata - Copywriter
Noah's Ark Communications

Mitch Defounga - Art Director
Noah's Ark Communications

Ezekiel Resedenz - Art Director
Noah's Ark Communications

4G- Portmanteau

CLIENT | **Airtel Nigeria**   AGENCY | **Noah's Ark**   AWARD | **Gold**

CREDITS

Lanre Adisa - Chief Creative Officer
Noah's Ark Communications

Eyo Ekeno - Chief Operating Officer
Noah's Ark Communications

Abolaji Alausa - Executive Creative Director
Noah's Ark Communications

Maurice Ugwonoh - Creative Director
Noah's Ark Communications

Baruch Apata - Copywriter
Noah's Ark Communications

Joba Popoola - Copywriter
Noah's Ark Communications

Ezekiel Resedenz - Art Director
Noah's Ark Communications

Mitch Defounga - Art Director
Noah's Ark Communications

FILM

Epa Ijebu

CLIENT | **Airtel Nigeria**   AGENCY | **Noah's Ark**   AWARD | **Silver**

CREDITS

Lanre Adisa - Chief Creative Officer
Noah's Ark Communications

Eyo Ekeno - Chief Operating Officer
Noah's Ark Communications

Abolaji Alausa - Executive Creative Director
Noah's Ark Communications

Maurice Ugwonoh - Creative Director
Noah's Ark Communications

Baruch Apata - Copywriter
Noah's Ark Communications

Joba Popoola - Copywriter
Noah's Ark Communications

Ezekiel Resedenz - Art Director
Noah's Ark Communications

Mitch Defounga - Art Director
Noah's Ark Communications

FILM

Doll Family

CLIENT | **Project Alert NG**   AGENCY | **Up In The Sky**   AWARD | **Silver**

CREDITS

Oje Ojeaga - Copywriter
Up In The Sky

Bolanle Akintomide - Producer
Up In The Sky

Omaga Idirigbe - Head, Creative
Up In The Sky

In-Laws - Gele

CLIENT | **Airtel Nigeria**   AGENCY | **Noah's Ark Communications**   AWARD | **Bronze**

CREDITS

Lanre Adisa - Chief Creative Officer
Noah's Ark Communications

Eyo Ekeno - Chief Operating Officer
Noah's Ark Communications

Abolaji Alausa - Executive Creative Director
Noah's Ark Communications

Maurice Ugwonoh - Creative Director
Noah's Ark Communications

Baruch Apata - Copywriter
Noah's Ark Communications

Joba Popoola - Copywriter
Noah's Ark Communications

Ezekiel Resedenz - Art Director
Noah's Ark Communications

Mitch Defounga - Art Director

In-Laws - Naming

CLIENT | **Airtel Nigeria**   **AGENCY** | **Noah's Ark Communications**   **AWARD** | **Bronze**

CREDITS

Lanre Adisa - Chief Creative Officer
Noah's Ark Communications

Eyo Ekeno - Chief Operating Officer
Noah's Ark Communications

Abolaji Alausa - Executive Creative Director
Noah's Ark Communications

Maurice Ugwonoh - Creative Director
Noah's Ark Communications

Baruch Apata - Copywriter
Noah's Ark Communications

Kunle Omope Copywriter
Noah's Ark Communications

Joba Popoola - Copywriter
Noah's Ark Communications

Ezekiel Resedenz - Art Director
Noah's Ark Communications

Mitch Defounga - Art Director
Noah's Ark Communications

Sky Sugar, Spice N' Sauce 2

CLIENT	**Good Business**
AGENCY	**Now Available Africa**
AWARD	**Gold**

CREDITS
Benjamin Anyan - Creative Director
Now Available Africa

Benjamin Anyan - Script Writer
Now Available Africa

Akwesi Agyekum - Animator/Editor
Now Available Africa

Yvonne Acheampong - Account Manager
Now Available Africa

Raise A Trophy

CLIENT I International Breweries Limited PLC   **AGENCY I** Culture Communications   **AWARD I** Silver

CREDITS

Yomi Benson - MD
Culture Communications

Akin Akingbola - Creative Director
Culture Communications

Clement Elebuwa - Copywriter
Culture Communications

Samuel Olonisakin - Group Head Creative/ Art Director
Culture Communications

Dare Okuntilu - Client Service Director
Culture Communications

Nathaniel Ogbu - Account Manager
Culture Communications

BRANDED CONTENT

| Wallflower

CLIENT **|** Accelerate TV   AGENCY **|** Accelerate TV   AWARD **|** Bronze

CREDITS

Michael Akinrogunde - Director/ Writer
Accelerate TV

Adenike Adebayo - Director/ Writer
Accelerate TV

Joel Adegboye - Director
Accelerate TV

Seun Richards - Writer
Accelerate TV

Charles Emere - Director/ Writer
Accelerate TV

Colette Otuseso - Executive Producer
Accelerate TV

Jite Ovueraye - Associate Producer
Accelerate TV

Kemi Akindoju - Producer
Accelerate TV

Bolanle Olosunde - Producer
Accelerate TV

Dara Ogunbowale - Production Manager
Accelerate TV

Timayo Ogunro - Production Manager
Accelerate TV

Lawrence Adejumo - D.O.P.
Accelerate TV

Ubong Ofong - Camera Man
Accelerate TV

Jerry Otor - Production Assistant
Accelerate TV

Mani Call Me

CLIENT | **Mentally Aware Nigeria Initiative (MANI)**   AGENCY | **Up In The Sky**   AWARD | **Silver**

CREDITS

Jessica Iwayemi - Copywriter
Up In The Sky

Olisa Ogbolu - Producer
Up In The Sky

Omaga Idirigbe - Head, Creative
Up In The Sky

DESIGN

I Shapeshifters Campaign

CLIENT **I X3M IDEAS**   AGENCY **I X3M IDEAS**   AWARD **I Bronze**

CREDITS

Steve Babaeko - Chief Creative Officer
X3M IDEAS

Adesola Akosoko - Creative Director
X3M IDEAS

Godwin Ndubuisi - Deputy Creative Director
X3M IDEAS

Femi Akowonjo - Senior Copywriter
X3M IDEAS

Kelechi Uduma - Copywriter
X3M IDEAS

Simi Ajayi - Copywriter
X3M IDEAS

Saturday Emmanuel - Motion Graphic Artist
X3M IDEAS

Israel Obatunde - Art Director
X3M IDEAS

Kimson Masters - Illustrator
X3M IDEAS

PITCHER FOR GOOD

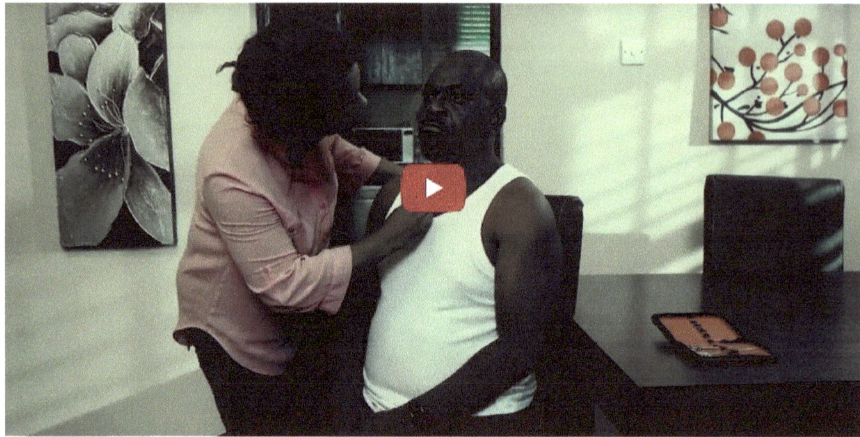

❙ Ruth

CLIENT ❙ Noah's Ark Communications   AGENCY ❙ Noah's Ark Communications   AWARD ❙ Good

CREDITS

Lanre Adisa - Chief Creative Officer
Noah's Ark Communications

Eyo Ekeno - Chief Operating Officer
Noah's Ark Communications

Abolaji Alausa - Executive Creative Director
Noah's Ark Communications

Maurice Ugwonoh - Creative Director
Noah's Ark Communications

Yemi Arawore - Creative Director
Noah's Ark Communications

Michael Gbolade - Deputy Creative Director
Noah's Ark Communications

Funsho Adebayo - Producer
Noah's Ark Communications

Kunle Omokpe - Copywriter
Noah's Ark Communications

Wole Aduwo - Director
Noah's Ark Communications

Background
According to a consultant psychiatrist in Nigeria, 25% of all women in Nigeria suffer from form of domestic abuse in their lifetime, but the society does not do enough to bring enlightenment to this trend, and some of the victims even make excuses for it. For the world Domestic violence day in 2018, we decide to do something about it.

Creative Idea
We used a combination of social and video to create Ruth, a story of a woman who was constantly battered by her partner. We anticipated a low response, and that was exactly what we got

Strategy
Our strategy was to test how sensitive Nigerians were to the issue, and then create a conversation that enlightens people about these issues, and pushes them to feel the pain of the victims of domestic violence, and for the victims to speak up.

Execution
With the low response, our strategy was in play. We followed up the social posts with a 6 minute film that showed in graphic detail, domestic abuse across YouTube, Instagram and Facebook

Results
-Over 13,000 views across YouTube, Facebook, and Instagram
-20% page growth for the Ruth twitter account, and increased participation in conversations
- More people were encouraged to speak up, and prevent fatalities

PITCHER FOR GOOD

Uncorrupt #GhanaSaysNo

Corruption is Ghana's most expensive canker. The country loses $3 Billion to it annually! But the worst part of corruption isn't the practice itself, but rather the social acceptance of it. In spite of all efforts, the Commission for Human Rights and Administrative Justice (CHRAJ) had failed to make people see how serious the canker is, get them to take a stand against it and influence government to take a tougher stance on it. This 'failure' became the brief we worked with.

We leaked a video of a teacher encouraging kids to be corrupt when they grow older. This enraged the country with nearly a million reactions on digital. A week later at the CHRAJ conference on international anti-corruption day, with the press, diplomats, top government officials, police and other leading civil servants in attendance we revealed CHRAJ's link to the teaser video. The point we made was: "If this upsets you, help us fight the actual menace; corruption."
We also premiered this emotional video that told actual corruption stories from the victims. Our TVC, radio and print ads were just as compelling. All traffic was directed to our website where visitors could read more about the campaign and get the #GhanaSaysNo filter.

We reached over 1 million people and got over $200K in earned media. But the biggest success of the campaign was the pressure it mounted on government to finally make the historic announcement of Ghana's first independent special prosecutor with the powers to investigate and prosecute anyone involved in corruption, even the president.

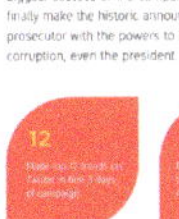

▎Uncorrupt Ghana Says No

CLIENT	▎	**Now Available Africa**
AGENCY	▎	**Now Available Africa**
AWARD	▎	**Good**

CREDITS

Benjamin Anyan - Creative Director
Now Available Africa

Colin Yesutor - Creative Director
Now Available Africa

Fuseini Isaac Addo - Production Manager
Now Available Africa

Kofi Mangesi - Project Lead
Now Available Africa

Basit Tahir Ibrahim - Copywriter
Now Available Africa

Akwesi Wierdu Agyeman - Videographer/Editor
Now Available Africa

Kofi Ocloo - Client Service Director
Now Available Africa

Dele Precious Emeka - Media Strategist
Now Available Africa

Background

Corruption is Ghana's most expensive canker. The country loses $3 Billion to it annually! But the worst part of corruption isn't the practice itself, but rather the social acceptance of it. In spite of all efforts, the Commission for Human Rights and Administrative Justice (CHRAJ) had failed to make people see how serious the canker is, get them to take a stand against it and influence government to take a tougher stance on it. This 'failure' became the brief we worked with and Uncorrupt #GhanaSaysNo was born.

Creative Idea

Ghana had just received her worst corruption score, there had been a series of high-profile corruption cases involving government organisations which seemed to lose sight of the suffering afflicted on the average Ghanaian. We wanted to give people a platform to share their stories in the build-up towards International anti-corruption day and work with advocates for change.

How did we make something so accepted, so disgusting? By equating corruption to crimes like rape and murder through Uncorrupt - #GhanaSaysNo

Strategy

We believed that #GhanaSaysNo would go viral. The target were decision makers, stakeholders in government and also those who had been affected by corruption in Ghana. A digitally lead campaign with integration of PR, press and TV we made use of WhatsApp, Facebook, Online News platforms, website as well as leveraging traditional.

Execution

How did we get the conversations started, we leaked the teacher Bismark teaser video on social media knowing the content was evoking enough to stir up conversations knowing that people would be outraged. at the CHRAJ conference on international anti-corruption day, with the world watching and national press and media (Citifm, MyJoyonline, GTV, MetroTV ect) diplomats, top government officials, police and other leading civil servants in attendance we revealed CHRAJ's link to the teaser video. The point we made was "If this upsets you, help us fight the actual menace; corruption." We followed this by launching emotional videos that told actual corruption stories from the victims, real stories from real victims of corruption this was adapted into the TVC. The radio's were just as compelling. This ignited conversations and debates on prime TV and Radio shows. In print ads we drew the comparison between corruption crimes which a blind eye is turned to that of murder or rape.

Results

We had opened the conversation about how normal Ghanaians were suffering as an effect of corruption and turned audience into advocates mounting pressure on the government to address issues relating to corruption in Ghana. The campaign went viral reaching over 1 million people and got over $200K in earned media. The biggest success of the campaign was that government finally made the historic announcement of Ghana's first independent special prosecutor with the powers to investigate and prosecute anyone involved in corruption, even the president.

2019 AGENCY OF THE YEAR
Noah's Ark Communications Lagos

2019 ADVERTISER OF THE YEAR
Union Bank PLC

LEARN THE SECRETS TO TAMING WILD IDEAS, SIGN-UP FOR OUR CREATIVITY PROGRAMME.
CULTURECODE
The virtual creativity school
www.culturecode.courses

PROGRAMMES INCLUDE:

FUTURE CREATIVE LEADERS ACADEMY

This is an intensive 3-day professional immersion programme for students in tertiary institutions. It is supported by the Advertising Practitioners Council of Nigeria (APCON). The Academy annually recognizes the best participating universities, lecturers and students. Winners in the FCLA competitions are sponsored to attend the Roger Hatchuel Academy in Cannes and the Dubai Lynx.

YOUNG PROFESSIONALS ACADEMY

The Young Professionals Academy is a bespoke learning programme for creative communications professionals of up to 30 years. In addition to the intensive learning opportunities, participants also engage in highly rewarding competitions like the Young Lions Competitions, where winners have the chance to represent their country in Cannes and the Young Pitcher Integrated Competition, where winners are sponsored to attend the Dubai Lynx.

CREATING A BETTER AFRICA

The Creating a Better Africa(CBA) Sustainability Programme is a high-profile career acceleration initiative for mid to senior level communications professionals. It is designed to inspire social purpose and sustainability as well as promote creativity as a catalyst for national development.

SEE IT BE IT AFRICA

See It Be It Africa is an extension of the Cannes Lions See It Be It initiative that addresses gender imbalance in creative leadership. The See It Be It Africa programme brings the message closer to more women in Africa.

PITCHER AWARDS

The Pitcher Awards celebrate outstanding work created or implemented in Africa across several categories including film, print, digital, media and PR.

PITCHER TALKS & WORKSHOPS

Pitcher Talks & Workshops present unique platforms for leading industry professionals to deliver top-notch seminars and conduct hands-on workshop sessions that focus on critical issues affecting the industry especially as it pertains to Africa.

Pitcher Festival of Creativity is organized by CHINI Africa, Cannes Lions official Festival Representative in Nigeria. For sponsorship, partnership or participation details, please send email to info@pitcherfestival.com

www.ingramcontent.com/pod-product-compliance
Lightning Source LLC
Chambersburg PA
CBHW040050240726
48664CB00004B/1133